POTTY TRAINING YOUR BABY

A Practical Guide for Easier Toilet Training

POTTY TRAINING YOUR BABY

Katie Van Pelt

AVERY PUBLISHING GROUP INC.
Garden City Park, New York

Cover design by Rudy Shur and Martin Hochberg
Cover photo © Dick Luria, NYC.
Illustrations by Jeff Jarka
In-house editor Jacqueline Balla

Library of Congress Cataloging-in-Publication Data

Van Pelt, Katie.
   Potty training your baby : a practical guide for easier toilet
training / Katie Van Pelt : (illustrations by Jeff Jarka).
      p.   cm.
   Includes index.
   ISBN 0-89529-398-6 (pbk.) : $6.95
   1. Toilet training.   I. Title.
HQ770.5.V36 1988   88-23681
649' .62--dc19   CIP

Printed in the United States of America

10 9 8 7 6

Dedication

To Steve, for making this happen.
To Tiffany, for making it possible.
To Joshua, for re-awakening the memories.
I love you.

Contents

Preface

As a young mother, I never quite understood how potty training could become such a hair-raising experience for parents. Unlike most people I know, all the children in my family were out of diapers before their second birthday. We just didn't have the problems that seem common in so many families.

After reading everything I could find about the subject and considering the advice offered by many doctors, I began to understand why problems develop. There is a general lack of information on the subject. Most of what parents find to read provides *outmoded* information that is too general and leaves many important questions unanswered.

For example, if a two year old refuses to participate, does it mean he's not ready to be trained? Or does it mean you're going about it the wrong way? Could it just be the child's way of expressing his independence? If a one year old pees on the potty whenever he's placed there and seldom wets his diaper, does it mean he's potty trained, or does he have potty-trained parents? Questions such as these create uncertainty for parents. Under the circumstances, even the most rational and intelligent parents can become unglued. It's little wonder that problems develop.

I believe potty training is more of a philosophy than a specific, step-by-step technique. This book presents some new thinking and general guidelines which will help you to potty train your child with minimal stress.

With an early start, my method enables you to finish training by the time a lot of parents are just beginning: by the age of one and a half to two years. But regardless of your child's age when you begin, the technique is much the same.

Ultimately, every baby will be potty trained. Every baby *wants* to be potty trained. It's human nature to strive for accomplishment and independence. The baby that is trained early is the one who receives complete support, encouragement and acceptance from his parents as training progresses. Potty training then becomes a rewarding, bonding experience for both you and your child, which is the way it was meant to be.

1

The Early-Start Alternative

Potty training is often one of the most frustrating aspects of parenting. For many, it's traumatic. For most, it's never over soon enough. But it doesn't have to be that way. Actually, potty training can be completed a lot sooner than most parents are led to believe. With the right approach, your child can be through with it about the time some say it should begin. It can also be a delightful experience.

The crucial concern for parents has always been *when* to start potty training. In the 50's and early 60's, leading experts advised waiting until a toddler was at least two years old before beginning. The belief was that a child had to be old enough to comprehend what training was all about and to understand the social connotations of it all. They also believed that, before any real attempt toward control could be made, the child's sphincter muscles had to be fully mature. At the time, this was thought to occur at approximately twenty-four months of age. Although some still abide by these guidelines, the old point of view is definitely changing. Potty training can begin as early as the child's first year.

We now know that sphincter development can occur much earlier (between the ages of one and one and a half years), and the argument that a young child lacks the comprehension to be trained has certainly lost credibility. Today, authorities in the field of child development recognize *it is really the parent's choice* whether to begin a child's training early or not. As long as a parent doesn't apply *pressure*, there now seems to be little expert objection to an early start.

Should parents decide to begin training early, they must be realistic. Potty training isn't accomplished quickly. There are no shortcuts. Early training starts with an emphasis on recognizing sensations and connecting those sensations with the appropriate muscles. Total control isn't possible until the sphincters have fully developed. Potty training is then completed once the child himself decides to take full responsibility. With an early start, this may happen at eighteen months, if you have an independent child. Or it may take longer, depending on the child's personality.

CHOICES

Early potty training is not a new concept. Generations past, it was most common for parents to potty train early and to do so successfully. Since every diaper soiled meant yet another to hand wash, there was ample incentive. Today, it's simply a matter of choice.

The standard approach is based on the child's ability to think about and take care of his own toileting needs from the very start of training. Success depends on a child's ability to understand and follow instructions. Training begins at approximately two years and can be expected to continue for another six to twelve months. Although most children complete their training by the time they are three years old, it is not uncommon to find children up to the age of four who are still wetting their pants.

Many parents find this approach to be frustrating because they recognize their child's readiness to start training as early as the first year. But at that age, they reason, a child can't follow instructions. Even at two years, some children simply can't or won't listen to potty training instructions.

This book provides a system that overcomes these problems. It is designed to meet the emotional needs of your child while teaching control at the same time. Training can begin before the first birthday and can be successfully completed by the second.

And it is easily adaptable for older toddlers, as well. This system removes the conflict that is so often found in potty training and allows it to become like any other "me-do" project for a child. It's not unlike learning to put socks on by himself. Once a process is observed and understood, a young toddler wants to do things for himself. To go to the potty unassisted is simply another avenue for self-expression. No pressure is required to complete potty training. A child does it naturally.

Of course, no child is going to master potty training right away. His sphincter muscles have to mature and he has to learn how to control them. The system detailed in this book puts your child in touch with muscles that he wouldn't ordinarily notice. Working at it daily, he will soon become aware of the physical sensations related to bowel and bladder control. This is where potty training really begins. With constant attention, those muscles will develop much more rapidly. And when the sphincter muscles are finally mature, your child can be in the final stage of potty training—instead of just beginning. With an early start, your child could be out of diapers well before the age of two.

DOES THE CHILD NEED TO KNOW WHAT IT'S ALL ABOUT?

Not necessarily. Control isn't the focus of early training; awareness is. Recognizing the body's inner workings is always the first step in training. During the early stages of potty training, a child's attention is centered on his body and its functions. Learning to control these functions comes later. Since control isn't an issue during the earliest phase of training, a baby who can sit up by himself is just as able to begin potty training as the toddler. By the time he's reached the second phase of his training, he will have already acquired a good understanding of his bodily functions and spent time exercising some control over them. Regardless of the child's age, the process is much the same.

INTUITIVE LEARNING

Many parents just don't understand how they could possibly teach their baby something that appears so complicated. But it's only complicated if you *think* it is. Teaching a baby is actually a lot easier than you'd imagine.

Babies do most of their communicating on an emotional level. A child "understands" things intuitively a lot sooner than he understands the words and actions attached to those things. So potty training is most successful when you interact with your child in the language he best understands—emotion.

Parents can easily see just how effective "emotional" communication can be. For example, look what happens when a toddler dances to show off for his parents. Mom and Dad laugh and clap their hands in amusement. And the baby dances all the more! Not a word has been spoken, yet the child intuitively knows that he is the star attraction and that his audience loves what he is doing. It is the parents' response that provides the incentive to keep on dancing. This same kind of emotional encouragement should be applied to potty training.

Obviously, you can't just sit a child down and explain that you want him to start peeing in the potty and expect it to happen. A baby won't understand this. Although he may already know what a wet diaper is, he may not recognize that he has the capability to purposely make it wet. He pees automatically, without any thought or effort.

Potty training involves more than simply teaching a child how to control a physical function. It is actually helping a child to recognize a series of physical sensations, to understand what those sensations mean, and then to control his urge long enough to get to the potty. You can't explain such sensations with words. You must take a different approach and help your child to make the associations and discover things *for himself.* The only way you can do this is on an emotional level.

The parents' attitudes and responses provide the key to early potty training. When you place the baby on a potty, your immediate response will tell him exactly what he needs to know. When he starts peeing and you become excited, he not only understands that this is *good*, but that it's also *fun!* If you do this consistently, within a short time he will purposely try to pee on the potty just to get that same, happy response from you. This puts him in touch with his body. In the beginning, the joy of sharing his accomplishment is really all the baby needs. A happy experience provides enough incentive for him to carry on.

A toddler may understand your request that he use the potty, but sometimes even that's not enough. If training has not yet begun, then he's accustomed to ignoring his body's functions. You're now asking him to control this impulse. A toddler may consider your request not only unnecessary, but a major inconvenience.

The toddler's emotional needs are quite different from a baby's because his priorities at this point in life involve the establishment of his autonomy. You can't ignore this fact. By providing him with ample opportunity to satisfy this emotional need, you'll be better able to gain a toddler's cooperation.

Babies Are Geniuses

Let's not underestimate a baby's capabilities. They are, by nature, very quick to absorb new experiences. But, first, opportunities must be presented. There's really no need to put off potty training until a child is old enough to *tell* you he's tired of wet diapers.

Realize that babies aren't incompetent beings. They simply lack experience. While a baby may not be able to totally control his little system, he can easily grasp the concepts.

THE BEST TIME TO BEGIN

Children enjoy learning new skills. They are most attracted to situations that provide a sense of challenge. Learning to walk, drinking from a cup, and feeding themselves all begin as an interesting challenge. The feelings of satisfaction that a child experiences each time he makes a little progress makes continued effort worthwhile.

A lack of challenge allows little opportunity to experience such feelings of accomplishment and is therefore a hindrance to any learning process. A child must have something to look forward to as he learns, something to satisfy his need for self-accomplishment. If a child is faced with a task that is below his current capabilities, the lesson will be perceived as boring and not worth the trouble.

This problem is demonstrated by the gifted child who fails in school. Learning isn't his problem; boredom is. If the child's superior abilities aren't noticed by the teacher, he may be judged as a failing student. The teacher will expect less of him and he, in turn, will meet those expectations and perform far below his potential. The teacher's attitudes and actions are transferred to the child. He soon begins to believe that her opinions of him are correct. If he sees himself as a failing student, then his performance level will remain far below his capabilities.

If the same child were to be placed in a more challenging environment, with a teacher who recognized his capabilities, he would respond differently. More favorable circumstances would allow him to take advantage of his natural abilities. He might easily become the star pupil in the class.

The same principle can be applied to potty training. Recognize what your child is capable of. Create a challenge that is attainable. Make it interesting and you'll create a training experience that encourages participation.

MUSCULAR MATURITY

The sphincter muscles control the bowels and bladder. Some doctors tell us they mature between twenty and twenty-four months of age. So, they say, it's useless to try to potty train any earlier. But this time frame is only an estimate. It is misleading because it represents the *latest* scale of development, not the average. It also implies that a child lacks any and all control over his system until complete development has occurred. This is absolutely false.

The average baby's nervous system has matured enough to

allow complete voluntary control of the sphincter muscles by the time he's reached eighteen months of age. Some babies complete this process as early as twelve months. For others, complete development may not occur before twenty-four months of age.

Since children's bodies develop at their own individual paces, this system is designed to work with the immature sphincter muscles as their natural maturing process continues. This training system encourages the development of the sphincter muscles to a degree, but nature completes the cycle. The only way you'll really know when the process is complete is when the training is over. At best, your observations will tell you that your child is making progress and gaining more control as time goes on.

IT TAKES TIME

It is important to remember that potty training cannot be completed until the sphincter muscles are fully mature, regardless of your child's age or the amount of training. However, it can be started much earlier because even immature sphincter muscles send out sensations. Because early training concerns itself entirely with recognizing these sensations, the lack of complete muscular development is unimportant.

Every physical thing a child does requires practice. Babies don't start walking around the house as soon as they learn to stand. Their muscles aren't developed enough. They take a few steps, then fall flat on their fannies. They hold on to Mom or Dad's fingers and slowly waddle across the room. With such little day-by-day efforts, they get better and better and their muscles become stronger and stronger. Soon, little feet are pattering all around the house. The same thing happens with potty training. Practice encourages the growth and maturing processes.

All babies go through the same stages and experiences while being trained. This process takes months, *regardless of the child's age.* A baby must learn what it feels like to be wet, to associate wetting with the muscles involved, to recognize the feelings of a bowel movement or the need to go to the potty. As the baby becomes aware of the muscles involved, he naturally begins to use them. The more often he does this, the more familiar he becomes with the muscles. The more familiar he is with the muscles, the more he will try to use them and the stronger those muscles become. As the muscles become stronger, he learns to control himself for longer and longer periods of time.

Once your baby is fully aware of all the sensations, he'll go on to the final stages of potty training. He'll learn to communicate his needs to you and, finally, to use his potty on his own. This last step is the *only* one that cannot occur until the sphincter muscles have completed their growth process. So instead of waiting until muscle development is complete before beginning, your child will already be in the final stages of training.

HELPING THE CHILD TEACH HIMSELF

One of the most fundamental aspects of potty training is consistently overlooked. That is the emotional gratification that motivates a child to try new experiences. Learning is as natural for a child as breathing. Learning comes easier if we provide an atmosphere of encouragement without making excessive demands. It is believed that we should provide enough stimulation and excitement for the child's mind to thrive, yet not so much that he becomes overwhelmed. We must achieve a balance. If we push too hard or expect more than he can deliver, he will withdraw, become frustrated, or angry.

You can't *force* a child to acquire a new skill. He learns because he is motivated to do so. He does this naturally, in a very spontaneous way.

A child motivates himself in many ways and, without interference, his inner drive serves as the catalyst for growth. Toddlers can be prompted to try just about anything if they are led to believe the activity is fun or interesting. They never sit and reason out a situation before trying it. They do not consider their limitations. They are drawn to experience life and everything it has to offer. We see examples of this constantly as we watch our children grow.

For example, a one year old may decide to start brushing his teeth because he sees his parents doing so. He wants to be like his parents; to be included in their rituals. He brushes his teeth to be like them, not because he wants to avoid cavities. His knowledge is much too limited to consider such things, but he is motivated to try. By trying, he learns. If his efforts are encouraged, the personal gratification he experiences will prompt him to try again. So teeth brushing will become a habit long before he learns the real reason why he's doing it.

PARENTS KNOW BEST

Ordinarily, parents are encouraged to stimulate their child's development in every area—physical and mental. But potty training seems to be the only area of development that is treated differently.

Many in the field of child development still regard potty training as an entirely physical process which the child must learn to control with logical decision-making. They believe that potty training shouldn't be started until around the second birthday, since the baby's mind must be mature enough to "think" about it first.

Pediatricians may be just as narrow-minded. Most doctors really don't give potty training much thought. It isn't uncommon for them to lack any firm opinions about it and to quickly pass over the subject with "off-the-cuff" advice. Most of their opinions are based on the belief that the child must be old enough to be "taught" with words and firm direction. This approach to training provides little incentive for the child. Since the toddler's emotional needs and development are totally overlooked, such a training experience becomes quite limited.

Unfortunately, many parents are willing to accept the myth that children under two are just too young to comprehend potty training. They'll ignore their own intuition and wait longer than necessary to begin potty training because some experts say it can't be done. As a result, we now have toddlers who are able to count and recite their ABC's, yet are still in diapers. It's one thing to delay training because you just don't care to get started. It's quite another to wait because you've received inadequate advice, leading you to believe that you don't have a choice in the matter. Because you do!

There is always more than one way to learn. One child, learning how to walk, will decide to hold on to furniture. Another will only walk in a walker. Another will demand a parent's finger to hold. There are various approaches to learning everything, yet potty training is considered a "one-way-only" learning experience.

Little human beings learn mostly by intuition, curiosity, observation and experience. They don't learn so much from words as they do from "feel." You communicate with them emotionally. You send them messages by your smiles, your tone of voice and your touch. Your attitude can influence their natural learning and self-discovery. And by taking a positive, realistic approach, you can help them to learn anything you want them to learn—like using the potty.

BETTER TO START SOONER THAN LATER

It's best to begin training at a time in the baby's development that compliments and encourages the early stages of training. This usually occurs well before the child's second year. For most children, it's even before the first birthday.

Nothing should be asked of the child that's not within his reach. On the other hand, don't handicap the child by underestimating his ability. As a baby, he may not be able to become totally trained, but he's certainly capable enough to begin.

The assumption that a child must be at least two years old to begin training is a mistake. By the second year a toddler is entering a period of development that makes training more difficult. The two year old is driven by a budding sense of independence that, at times, overwhelms both him and his parents. He's argumentative and contrary. He doesn't want to be reminded that there are things that he still doesn't know. He much prefers to believe that he knows all he needs to know. The growing awareness that he is a separate being with a mind of his own must constantly be tested. Two year olds want to assert themselves. To the toddler, potty training is just another situation that must be "handled." His instinct is to dig in his heels and holler, just to make a point.

By two years of age, he has missed the most ideal time to begin, or to accept, the idea of potty training. To expect a rambunctious two year old to stop what he's doing to sit on the potty is actually going against his grain. For the pleasant, submissive stage is over.

This isn't to imply that training a toddler is impossible—only that certain problems are more likely to develop. His behavior is shifting from dependency to that of independence. Since he can't be expected to handle his needs on his own, he must constantly ask for help. This is something a two year old often finds difficult to do. After all, being in control is most important at this time. Asking for assistance means giving up that control.

This situation can be avoided when you begin a child's training when he's younger. Then you're dealing with an entirely different situation. The developmental stage compliments the early steps of potty training. In the first year, the average child has become particularly interested in other people and their responses to his behavior. He tries to imitate behavior and takes pride in his achievements. He loves the company of his parents and their involvement in his activities.

By twelve months, he's fully aware of his audience. He likes to repeat performances that generate excitement and laughter. He enjoys the social give-and-take. He's learned to anticipate attention, excitement and praise when he does something new or special. His parents are the major influence in his life, which suits him just fine. He's cooperative because it is the only way he knows how to be.

These are the attributes that allow potty training to go most smoothly because you are asking the child to do something that is natural for him at this stage of development. He is thrilled to participate, and learning about his body delights him. When you potty train your child in a gentle, relaxed manner, he is blessed with the best possible experience. Progress comes gradually. As it does, the child's self-confidence and sense of identity are enhanced. His frame of mind encourages curiosity and participation in the training.

By the time he enters a more independent stage, he'll be in a position to put what he's learned about himself into action. He will complete his own training by his own initiative, not yours. The focal point of training is not to obtain quick control. The main point is to encourage the child to *want* to take control of his body, which he does in an easy and relaxed way.

2

Basic Elements Needed

There's a process, a method to potty training that can be broken down into three segments. Training begins by first helping a child to recognize a series of physical sensations and to understand what they mean. The second step is helping him to connect those sensations with the appropriate muscles and practicing with them. Finally, he learns purposeful control of his functions until complete control is achieved.

The first two steps involve experiencing and recognizing the body's functions. This is where the bulk of your child's training takes place. It doesn't happen overnight. Progress comes in small steps. Regardless of age, a child cannot move into the final stage of training until he has a full understanding of his body. And while this part of training takes the most time, a child does not have to intellectually understand the process in order to learn from the experience.

There are four elements necessary in order for training to begin. These are: a healthy baby, a baby who is capable of sitting up by himself, a relaxed attitude and a sturdy potty.

A HEALTHY BABY

Do not try to potty train a sick baby. If your child is having health problems, it is best for everyone involved to delay potty training. When a person feels bad physically, it's very easy to become upset. If a toddler becomes irritated at having to deal with the potty when he doesn't feel well, he may develop a negative mind set. This is the very thing that you want to avoid. New learning experiences require confidence, desire and energy. Illness depletes these natural attributes. If your child is ill, put the potty away until another day.

If your child has experienced serious health problems, don't begin training until the entire convalescent period is over.

A BABY CAPABLE OF SITTING UP BY HIMSELF

You can't begin training until your baby is able to sit up all by himself. He should be able to sit for at least thirty minutes without having to rely on the extra support of his hands or props. If your child sits in a slumped position, leaning sideways or forward, then he's not yet ready for potty training.

The ability to sit is determined mostly by the back and abdominal muscles. In a baby's development, this can occur as early as five months. But some babies don't sit up until the ninth month or later. Under no circumstances should you consider beginning potty training before this time. These muscles must be sufficiently developed to easily support and steady his upper trunk as he sits on the potty.

Starting training before the baby can sit confidently by himself could magnify his natural fear of falling and losing control. So let your baby master sitting before you begin putting him on the potty.

A RELAXED ATTITUDE

The attitude we take toward anything we do directly affects the success of our effort. *A relaxed and positive attitude on your part is the most important element in successful potty training.*

A child learns best in an atmosphere that is free of anxiety. Surely the world is an imperfect place, and nobody lives in an entirely stress-free environment. There is stress even in the most perfect of homes. But potty training is an area of development that needs special attention. We must be careful to avoid unnecessary stress. Keep cool, no matter what happens.

Don't pay much attention to the potty training advice of other people. Unwise or out-moded theories can often create real stress for parents. Everyone has an opinion about potty training that they can't wait to pass on to you. They always seem to know more about what you *can't* do than what you *can*. But few people are really aware of the facts, and most of their second- and third-hand theories are wrong. So try to maintain your emotional balance and ignore any negative ideas that may hinder your progress.

It's Not A Contest

Stress and anxiety can also be created when parents feel that their child's accomplishments (or lack of them) are a reflection of their parenting abilities. This thinking is not only wrong, but it creates conflict between parent and child.

Don't let the training become some kind of contest. We live in a highly competitive society in which contests and games play an important role in our social development. Certainly, our children's physical accomplishments are sources of great pride. Parents love to brag about how "quickly" their baby does something and how smart he is. And that's okay. But when taken a step too far, pride may actually become a catalyst for anxiety. Don't allow potty training to become your child's first "failure."

Yes, early potty training is certainly something to be proud of. But it's not a contest. That's not the point at all. A child doesn't "win" by finishing earlier than anyone else. If you allow yourself to become a judge, a referee or a "scorekeeper," you will do more harm than good.

Understand that potty training means more to a child than just mastering his toilet needs. Potty training is a child's first, true self-image experience. All aspects of training influence the child's awareness of himself and provide a sense of his place in the world. How he perceives his body and himself when he's older is often dictated by the experiences he has during training. The ramifications are broad, complex and life-long.

We all have our own emotional baggage, the roots of which began at infancy. Since training usually covers a period of six months to one year, many impressions can be implanted in your child's mind. Try to make them positive ones.

Remember that the elimination of wastes is an entirely normal and healthy process. Babies don't have negative feelings about these functions unless *you* create them. Learning to sit on the potty should be a pleasure, not an ordeal, and certainly not a judgment of success or failure. If the experience is a positive one, your child will be free to develop a more confident attitude towards himself. This positive self-image will follow him into adulthood.

Of course, every child perceives these experiences on different levels and you can only do so much to enhance your child's self-image. However, you can avoid creating harmful, unnecessary problems. If you maintain a positive attitude about everything connected with potty training, you can help him to become a more emotionally well-balanced person.

SELECTING THE RIGHT POTTY

The selection of a potty is very important. Many different styles are available, and a wrong choice could present problems. For example, many models are unsteady and can easily tip over. Others are designed for a small child and allow no room for growth. Most models have detachable splatter cups, but some don't allow the cup to be locked into place. So the child may constantly pull the cup up and out and pee over the rim—and onto the floor!

Take your child with you when you go to buy a potty. Sit him on different models and make sure the fit is right. There should be plenty of room for future growth on the sides and behind the baby's bottom. Remember—babies grow quickly, and that should be taken into consideration as you make your final choice.

Most of today's models are constructed entirely of plastic. The most unsteady ones have straight sides and/or a narrow base. When the child leans just a bit too far to the left or right,

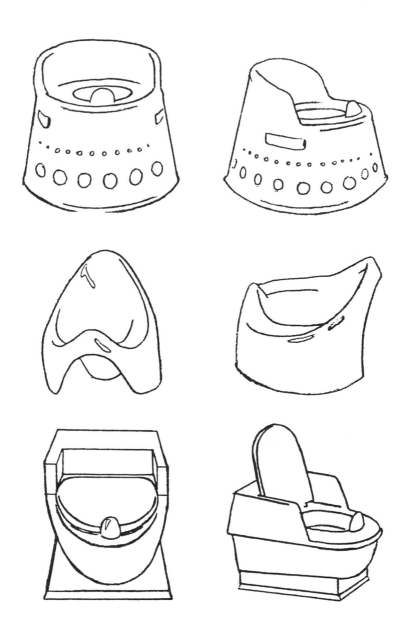

Various Types of Flare-Bottomed Potties (Front and Side Views)

the whole thing can easily flip onto its side. Narrow-based potties are an open invitation to disaster. If you decide on a "commode" model, buy one that's constructed with a wider rim of plastic around the base (which flares out to give more stability).

Some models are built to resemble a little chair with a hole in the seat. Unless it is made with extra supports across the base, it will not be steady enough for a toddler to use safely. Regardless of the style you're considering, sit your child on the potty. Lean his body in all directions to see if the base has any tendency to lift off the floor.

Avoid armrests. When the baby leans to one side, he holds the armrest (which exerts extra leverage). This makes the chair exceptionally easy to tip over. In addition, the armrests make the act of sitting down on the potty more precarious. Babies simply don't sit down on these things without using their hands. They grab the armrest as they are backing onto the chair to sit. Unless they grab both armrests and back straight onto the chair (something few babies are capable of doing), they can flip the chair onto its side even before their fanny hits the seat. A baby only has to have this happen once before deciding that the thing is more trouble than it's worth. If you want a chair-like model, find one that has a broad base with very sturdy legs. Also keep in mind that the heavier it is, the better.

The best potties are more rounded and shaped like an inverted, rounded cone. The base is circular and much wider than the upper half, where the child sits. No matter how far the child leans, the potty stays firmly in place on the floor.

Some potties offer a built-in music box. This is supposed to keep the baby interested and entertained as he sits on it. That's okay, I suppose. But the problem is that the music box is usually positioned behind the child's back. So the first thing the child does when the music starts to play is to twist out of his sitting position to investigate the box. Little people love gadgets, but having one on a potty diverts attention from the potty training to the potty itself.

You'll also find models designed with a removable seat section that may be placed on an adult toilet. This is a great idea, if it works as it's supposed to. The instructions on the box give the impression that all you have to do is snap the potty top on and off whenever you want. I bought one of these, thinking how simple it would be! Only I found the lid nearly impossible to remove from the potty. My husband couldn't even pull the thing off! We eventually had to use tools to take off what had been advertised as an "easy-to-remove" seat. It turned out to be just as difficult to put back on as it was to get off. So be sure to check everything over carefully before you buy.

When selecting a potty, always examine the splatter cup. Girls as well as boys will need this piece attached to the potty. When the cup is in place, make sure it fits comfortably between your child's legs. The cup itself should not press into the baby's groin area. If you can place a finger between the cup and the baby without touching either one, then the fit is right. If you can't, then the fit is too snug.

You will find seat straps available on many models. They give the impression that the baby is safer, but that's actually a misconception. Any potty can be tipped over by an active baby who wants to get *up*. If the straps are fastened when the baby stands, the potty will go with him. Besides, a baby perceives being tied down as a form of punishment. You certainly don't want him to have that kind of feeling about his potty!

Finally, remember never to turn your back on a small baby sitting on the potty. Accidents happen in the blink of an eye, so be careful.

Why Buy A Potty—Won't The Toilet Do?

Unless you are training an older toddler, the answer to this question is *no*. Trying to use a full-size toilet at the beginning of training creates too many problems. The reasons are understandable. The most obvious is that the toilet was designed to accommodate an adult's body. From a tot's point of view, a toilet's size can be very intimidating.

If you want your child to be able to use both the potty *and* the toilet, I would advise purchasing a separate potty top in addition to the potty. These are inexpensive and can be found wherever potty chairs are sold. But don't substitute a potty chair top

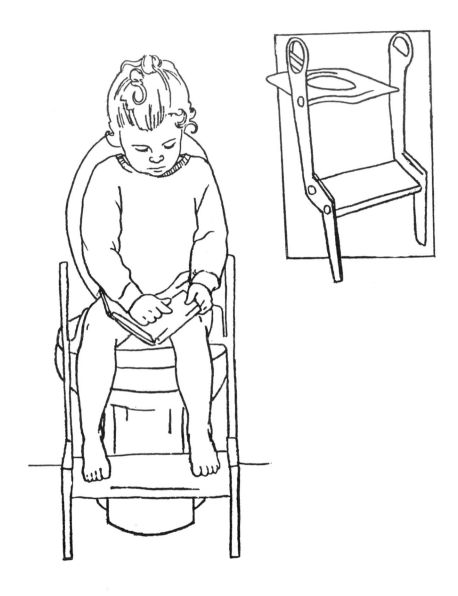

Child Using A Step-Up Ladder

that can be placed on an adult toilet for a real potty. They're okay for travel use and in the later stages of your child's training, but aren't a suitable replacement for his own potty.

Your child needs a potty he'll be able to master all by himself. He should have a potty that he's able to sit on comfortably and with ease. This helps him to develop confidence and encourages him to proceed to the final stages of training.

For a small child, the thought of using a regular toilet without assistance is unrealistic. An adult toilet can deny him the feeling of self-competence. Without this, potty training is far more difficult to achieve. Such frustration is counter-productive to the training process.

After your child has made good progress on his own little potty, then he can begin using the adult toilet, perhaps with the aid of a step-up ladder. By this time, his sense of balance will be perfected. The toilet routine will be "old hat," so you won't have to worry about it (and neither will he).

Where To Put The Potty

When you first bring the potty home, put it in the room where your baby spends the most time. He'll be more comfortable and at ease there. It doesn't have to be in the bathroom. In fact, the bathroom might be counter-productive in the early stages of potty training. Bathrooms are places of amazement for a baby, filled with exciting colors, smells and objects that can easily divert his attention from you and the job at hand. You want him to focus on his body sensations and his potty, not on the shower curtain, towels or soap dish.

There will be plenty of time to move the potty into the bathroom. For now, a familiar place will work more to your advantage. If that happens to be the den or the living room, don't worry about comments from visitors. When you explain why it's there, guests will understand and probably be amused. If not, it's their problem, not yours.

3

The One Year Old

Babies are a lot smarter and more capable than most people imagine. They are also highly impressionable. The way you approach a child during potty training affects the way he'll begin to feel about himself deep within. So to have the best possible training experience, to make it progress easily, you must create an atmosphere where babies have fun as they learn and gain competence, where pride and achievement can be displayed daily.

Potty training should offer a baby the added enjoyment of dazzling his parents by his very existence. The training should encourage a child to express himself fully, without fear of criticism. Negative reinforcements (scolding, guilt trips) should never enter into the training process. Bit by bit, these parental negatives chip away a child's confidence and sense of self-worth. In such case, training takes longer to complete and is usually beset by problems.

With a stress-free method of potty training, you avoid the problems usually associated with early training. This system provides the guidelines necessary to boost the sense of pride and accomplishment that is so necessary for a child's emotional well-being. In many ways, it may be said that this system gives the child the opportunity to potty train himself—and to do so at a very early age.

PHILOSOPHY

Potty training is a big experience for babies and toddlers. It's much more than a physical activity. It contributes to their emotional development, as well. With proper guidance, potty training will provide the building blocks for your child's self-esteem and encourage a better self-image. So *how* you interact with your child is of fundamental importance. If you demand more from your child than he can deliver, you are setting the stage for disappointment. This erodes his self-confidence and slows down the training. With positive experiences, a child learns that he is *important* and that he can *control his environment*.

A child's behavior mirrors his self-image. When he feels good about himself, he becomes more involved, more outgoing and less threatened. He learns to trust himself and others. A positive and enlightened atmosphere will always bring out the best in your child and will enhance the entire potty training experience.

Your goal is to guide your child in such a way that he can discover how his body works. During the process, he'll gain valuable experience as he experiments with his body. By the time he reaches the point where his sphincter muscles are completely developed, he will be fully capable of finishing his training.

As training progresses, always consider what developmental phase your child is in. Since babies and toddlers pass through different stages at different times, it is up to you to recognize your child's emotional and physical needs and to stay in tune with him. He's maturing and changing almost daily. Adjust yourself to your child as he grows. The training experience should never be allowed to become mundane or boring.

Once a child has become accustomed to the fundamental aspects of training, introduce him to some of its responsibilities. Allow him to actively participate in the decision-making. For example, ask him if he'd like to drop the wet diaper in the diaper pail. At first, you'll have to answer "yes" for him, but he'll soon get the idea. Ask him if he will carry the diaper for you as you take it to the pail. Let him drop it in. As soon as a child begins to walk, allow him to dispose of his wet diaper by himself. If he doesn't want to carry it to the pail, ask him if he wants you to do it for him. This keeps him involved and stimulates his sense of power and accomplishment.

Whenever possible, let him fetch a new diaper for you when he needs a change. When you begin to help him onto the toilet, if you have more than one in your home, allow him to choose which one he will use next. Allow him to flush the toilet with every opportunity that comes his way. When he gets into training pants, buy them in different colors and let him decide which color he wants to wear.

Little girls should be encouraged to wipe after wetting as soon as they begin to walk. They love this kind of participation. Since tots like to imitate, don't be concerned if your son wants to wipe after peeing, as well. Let him. It's no big deal.

Don't limit yourself to the suggestions provided in this book. Use your imagination while training your child. Encourage his involvement. It really isn't easy being a little kid. Everyone seems to be constantly bossing them around. As a child approaches fifteen or sixteen months old, he becomes very aware of this and recognizes his vulnerability. This, in itself, causes a child to become rebellious. By allowing him to make choices, you help to alleviate some of his tension. You benefit from this just as much as he does. Training runs more smoothly and ends earlier simply because your child participates and is taught to assume control. Your encouragement lifts a child's self-esteem. Most importantly, it lets the child know that you have faith in his ability, that you trust and respect him.

Potty training is an educational experience. To approach it in any other way would be wrong. It doesn't matter how old the child is—learning takes time. As with all physical tasks, children progress at their own pace. All you can do is provide the proper setting with your support, your encouragement and, most of all, your respect. The rest is up to him.

The following guidelines are simple to follow. This technique eliminates trauma, anger or pain for both the parent and child. Whether you're beginning your child's training at nine months or at two years, the bottom line is that *potty training should be a time of bonding, learning and enjoyment.*

BEGINNINGS

Potty training can actually start as soon as a baby is able to sit up on his own and remain sitting for a good while without support. This is actually the most natural time for the baby to begin. At this age, babies are quite limited in their ability to get around. They are very limited in the amount of things they can do. They depend on you to take them from one room to another, to give them their favorite toy, to entertain them. You are the gateway to all their new experiences. The new things that you show them are received with open joy and curiosity.

For the baby who has just recently mastered sitting on his own, getting to sit up on a potty is terrific fun. Babies are usually very eager to "show their stuff" and are filled with pride as they do so. With a happy and relaxed attitude on your part, you set the foundation for effective potty training.

THE TRAINING EXPERIENCE

Babies commonly wet approximately twenty minutes after having their milk. Like most adults, they also pee immediately after waking from sleep.

For the first three or four weeks, try to catch your baby just before the act. Place him on the potty immediately after he wakes from a nap and twenty minutes after he drinks his milk. Sit him there for only two or three minutes. As you wait, hold his attention by talking to him and giving him a small object to play with (however, no food while on the potty, please).

Make it a quiet time of gentle communication between the two of you. If and when he pees in the potty, show your excitement. Point out to him that he is wetting *while he is doing so*. He'll react to your joy and will soon realize just what it is he's doing that is causing all your excitement!

My daughter, who is now seventeen, was completely potty trained at eighteen months. Although I certainly helped her with wiping, I no longer had to take her to her potty. She went on her own. I started Tiffany's training early by placing her on her new potty twenty minutes after she finished nursing. Much to my delight, the first time I put her on the potty, she started to pee. I started hopping around, acting like a clown, laughing and pointing into the potty and saying "pee-pee." To another adult, I'm sure I might have looked ridiculous, but she loved the show. I let her look at the pee in the potty, then we took it into the bathroom and flushed it. And though she may not have understood all I was saying, I told her exactly what we were doing each step of the way. We repeated this scenario three times each day.

Of course, she didn't always wet, but when she did, I went into my clowning routine. By the end of the first week, whenever I put Tiff on the potty, she would concentrate so hard her little face would turn red as she strained to pee. The second she started, she'd look my way and give the biggest grin. She wanted me to clown and dance around the room, which I promptly did. It was great fun. My playful approach made peeing in the potty a game. The game encouraged her own playfulness and created a very receptive attitude. This also gave her total control over the situation, which presented her with an opportunity she simply could not resist. There were no expectations, no pressure— only fun.

That was our beginning. So within that first week, she discovered the muscles which make bladder control possible and started focusing her attention on them.

Always remember that a pleasant attitude must be maintained. Potty training should be fun. Babies love to learn. They love little games and they love to do things that get positive reactions from Mom and Dad. If your child sees that you're having a good time, he's more likely to get into the spirit of it all. Your good, playful attitude is transferred to the baby. As a result, the learning process is speeded up, and the baby gets trained much sooner.

Pacing and Patience

During these first few weeks, it's very important to go slowly. Keep diapers dry. Check often and change the diaper as soon as he wets or "poops." The primary reason for this is so your child can make simple comparisons between the feel of wet and dry.

When changing your baby, talk to him. Tell him you're chang-ing his diaper because this one is wet or "poopy." Tell him this as a point of information, never with even a hint of disapproval. Also bring it to his attention whenever he passes gas. This will focus his attention on yet another of his body's functions.

As you do all this, you're acquainting your child with his body. In essence, you're helping to develop his whole attitude toward the potty and toilet training. You want it to be a totally positive experience. Make it a fun, sharing experience.

Don't Fight

Potty training should never become a war of wills. *Don't pressure your child for results.* If you do, he'll develop an attitude problem. Imagine how you'd feel if someone dictated when and where you'd go next, hovering over you all the while, waiting. Babies are people, too! Always treat your child with respect. Keep in mind that you're dealing with his self-esteem here. If he doesn't have to pee, then accept that. Take him off the potty and tell him he didn't pee as you put his diaper back on. Furthermore, make sure he knows that *it's okay when he doesn't!* The more supportive your attitude, the more enjoyable the whole experience will be for your baby.

Always take into consideration how the day is progressing for your child. If he's overly tired, fussy from lack of sleep, or both-ered by teething, then skip sitting him on the potty. If family or guests are visiting and the normal routine has been disrupted, then wait until the next day to resume training.

Talk To Your Baby, Explaining It All

Talk to your child whenever you're helping him with his toilet needs. Ask him if he has to pee before taking him to the potty. Tell him you're taking his diaper off so he can pee on the potty. Tell him you're changing his diaper because he's wet or has pooped. As he pees on the potty, tell him what's happening. If he sits on the potty and nothing happens, tell him so. Express your pleasure when he does go, but remember to tell him it's okay when he doesn't. Be his friend. Tell him all about it. He won't understand what you're saying at first, but he will soon enough.

Once your child understands the meaning of your words, he may sometimes get a little ahead of himself. Many a parent can relate the story of approaching their dry baby, telling him it's time to pee, then finding a warm wet diaper upon arriving at the potty. This isn't a real problem, just a mis-cue. The baby did exactly what was asked of him—he just did it too soon! If this happens to you regularly, don't mention the key words "pee" or "potty" until the diaper is off. Words become signals, and mis-understandings come easy for small children. If you change your phrasing, the problem should disappear in no time.

Stepping Up Training

Babies progress at their own individual paces. Remember that your child will not necessarily need to pee simply because you are placing him on his potty. Watch him carefully and be en-couraging, but don't try to push ahead too quickly. As he be-comes acquainted with his potty, and begins to use it fairly regu-larly, you can begin to step things up a bit.

Start putting your baby on the potty at *twenty-minute intervals during the day.* Ask him if he needs to pee. Then tell him what you are doing to help him each time. The phrases you use will quickly be remembered and understood. And you will soon be pleasantly surprised to find him indicating either a "yes" or a "no" in his own little way when you ask him if he needs to pee.

Initially, you need to follow this twenty-minute schedule for only two or three hours a day. As you work with your child, you'll learn his habits and be able to catch him with amazing accuracy. This will enable him to more fully associate the proc-ess of removing the diaper, then sitting on the potty to pee. Be observant. Watch for clues that indicate it's time to go to the potty.

Once you learn his schedule, you can adjust the twenty-min-ute interval to suit him. Some babies have an innate ability to hold their urine for quite some time. As soon as you are aware

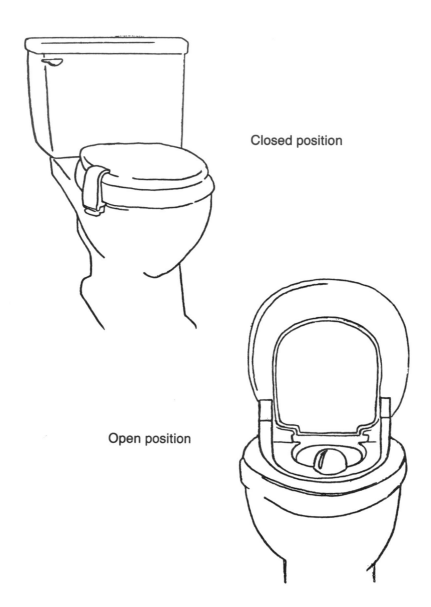

Closed position

Open position

Toilet Seat Lock

A good device to prevent your child from playing with toilet water.

of his pattern, approach him approximately five to ten minutes before he would ordinarily wet.

If he doesn't pee, simply tell him so as you take him off the potty. Then try again ten or fifteen minutes later. After all, you aren't making a demand for performance from your child— you're giving him an opportunity. Always show your approval with each accomplishment. *Never put pressure on the baby. Never show disappointment.*

Sleeping Patterns May Change

As potty training progresses, your child may experience some problems sleeping at night. His bladder is small, and as he gains more control of it, he'll often wake up instead of peeing in his sleep. Some babies do this more than others. At this point in the training, many babies start to wet, then hold in the rest and cry out for help. These are indications that the child is beginning to gain more voluntary control of his sphincter muscles, even though they have not yet completed their development.

If he does wake up at night and his diaper is dry or only a little wet, place him on his potty without delay. He'll probably be quite fussy since he's not fully awake, so be especially gentle and reassuring. If he doesn't pee quickly after you sit him on the potty, put the diaper back on and lull him back to sleep. This restlessness shouldn't last long, so be patient. Soon, he'll remain dry until morning—just like you.

Let Your Child Learn By Watching

As you're potty training your baby, remember you are also introducing him to one of the most fascinating things in your house: the toilet. Let your child go with you into the bathroom when you dump his potty into the toilet. Let him flush it. Let him see that you use this big potty, too. Let him flush the toilet after you use it. Tell him all about it!

Toilets are great fun. But be aware that they can also be dangerous. Babies love to splash their hands in the toilet water and also enjoy seeing their own reflections in it. Don't be mad, but do teach your baby that *toilets are not for play*. They have only one purpose. Make a habit of closing all toilet lids after each use. There have been cases where babies have actually fallen into the toilet head first and drowned. This is one mistake no one should have to suffer the consequences of.

Your baby will probably develop a fascination with his own potty, especially if it has a lid. This is normal and is part of the learning experience. Keep the potty very clean and let the child play with it as much as he likes. But be aware that little fingers can sometimes get pinched by the lid. If this happens often, lay the potty on its side until he's better able to manage.

When Baby Starts To Take Over

Within a few months, your baby will have it all figured out. He won't have complete control of his sphincters, but he will know when it's about time to go. He may want to tell you it's potty time, but be unable to say the words. This can be frustrating for a baby and can make him suddenly cranky. Anyone gets upset when they've "got to go" and can't get to the bathroom. So when your baby starts fussing, it could be his way of saying "potty time."

By this time, your child should clearly understand you when you talk about the potty. So when he turns fussy, ask him if he's got to go. He may indicate that's exactly what he wants. If so, get him there quickly.

Sometimes you'll get mixed signals. A baby may be fussing because his bladder is full, but won't want to take the time to have his diaper taken off, then have it put back on again. He knows this routine and it can get a little boring. To him, it seems like a long time to wait around before getting back to play. So when he's fussing and you ask if he needs to pee and he gets even fussier, he may not mean "no." He may mean "yes, I've got to go but I'm not pleased about it 'cause I was having fun and now I've got to stop while you work with my diaper!" You'll have to use your intuition to figure out when "no" really means "yes."

Help your baby onto his potty immediately as soon as he ex- hibits a need during the day. Always show your child that you're there for him. This encourages him to communicate with you all the more. Monitor his schedule because it will lengthen quickly as he grows. Take potty breaks as soon as you think you've gotten one of his cues.

However, if he begins to protest on the way to the potty, respect his wishes. You don't want sitting on the potty to feel like a form of punishment. Even if he ends up wetting or messing his diapers a few minutes later, don't let it upset you. You are still making progress. He did hold it in for a while, after all. Those muscles are getting stronger. He's learning.

Down and Out

Now let's talk about how you should empty the potty. For the younger baby, just empty it into a regular toilet, saying "Let's put [whatever it is he did] in the big potty." Most kids love to watch the toilet water flush, so take your child with you as you empty and flush. When they see that they're participating by contributing whatever it is that's being flushed, they become even more fascinated. However, once this enthusiasm grabs hold of your baby, he'll start trying to put anything and everything into the toilet. So keep a close eye on him.

Some children are frightened by the sound of the toilet flushing. They might even begin to associate this fear with bladder and bowel movements. I've never seen such a child myself, but if it happens to your child then don't dispose of the waste in his presence. Give him time, and then begin to occasionally flush the unused toilet. The problem will soon resolve itself.

Most babies take a special delight in flushing the toilet. As soon as your child is able to reach the handle and has the strength to make it flush, let him do it whenever he's around. You may also let him turn off the light as you exit the bathroom. This gives him more to experience, a sense of power and accomplishment. Again, encourage your child to keep you company in the bathroom. Be happy, and let him see that all is well.

As your toddler gains experience, he'll probably want to empty his potty himself. Rather than discourage him, let him take his potty to the toilet. Don't turn it into a negative, "you can't" situation. Stay close to avoid any spills, but let him do it himself.

On To Training Pants

Once you have confidence that your baby has progressed sufficiently, you'll begin to move from diapers to training pants. There are several types of panties your child can wear. Styles that offer three-, four- or five-ply protection are best. Single-layer terrycloth panties shouldn't be used until your child has reduced his number of accidents to a minimum, since they provide the least absorbency.

Make sure the panties you buy are big enough for your child to easily pull down by himself. You don't want your child to become frustrated because his panties are stuck! If they are too snug over the hips, they'll bunch up as your child tries to pull them down. Pay particular attention to the leg openings. There should be enough elastic for ample stretch. If possible, try a pair on your child to be sure.

Since an "accident" in training pants will also wet the floor, it's best for your child to start wearing them for short periods when you are nearby. If you're going to be too busy to quickly drop what you're doing to get him to the potty, then keep the diaper on. Or you may want to put plastic panties over the training pants.

As you begin to use training pants, you also begin to tell your child there are "correct" and "incorrect" places to pee. By now, your child will clearly understand all the language associated with this process. When you find a wet panty, take it off and replace it with a diaper. As you do so, explain carefully that "you are not supposed to pee in the panty. You are supposed to pee in the potty. You wet this panty, so we have to put a diaper on."

When you put the diaper on, do so in a positive, matter-of-fact manner. Don't let it be seen as punishment. Tell your child he must put a diaper on because his underwear got wet, as if it's no big deal to you. This lets your child know that his actions dictate whether he gets to wear a panty or a diaper. It gives your tot a sense of control. Training pants feel "neat," and toddlers like them. If he wets the panty and has to shift back into the diaper each time, he'll come to recognize that if he had gone to the potty, he'd still have the "reward" of wearing his new training pants. This will stimulate his growing sense of independence and will encourage him to take on more and more responsibility for his own actions.

Babies can get out of panties long before they can get back into them, so you'll sometimes find your baby playing bare-bottomed. Upon inspection you'll often find that the potty has been used without your being aware of it. And sometimes your child will call you to the potty to see he's done it all by himself. Make a big deal out of this! Really show your child how happy and proud you are of him.

Sometimes a child will dump his potty all by himself. He may even spill some of the contents on the floor. Be careful not to blow your top if this happens. Remember—he was only trying to do the right thing!

After your child has used the potty alone several times in a row, stop taking him to it *unless he comes to you* for help first. Let him do it on his own for as long as he can. Expect to have some accidents during the next few weeks. It's not uncommon for a child to call you to show where he made a puddle. If this occurs, explain that it was an accident. Talk about it, but don't lose your cool. Help him into a clean pair of pants and clean up the mess. Then, *do not* refer to the accident again. It's over. Move ahead and don't make it an issue.

When your child consistently lets you know when he needs to get on the potty and the "accidents" are less frequent, you can start using training pants exclusively, except when your child is sleeping. (You may want to use a plastic panty over the training pants for extra peace of mind.)

If your child begins to have more than a few accidents, then take control of the situation again and go back to the "if you wet your panty, we have to put a diaper on" system for a while. When he begins to assert himself once again, allow him to continue on his own.

Soon your baby will finalize his training on his own. You'll still need to help out with wiping and getting pants up, along with occasional reminders. But eventually, you'll be able to toss out those diapers for good. Just remember—always approach the potty training with good cheer, applause, love and a good dose of respect.

STARTING LATER

If you're starting to potty train a baby of eighteen months, your approach should basically be the same as with a baby of seven or eight months—with one difference. A toddler of this age will have greater bladder control and storage capacity. After your child has had a bottle, wait about forty minutes before going to the potty. Then extend the time between trips to the potty from forty minutes to an hour. Try to avoid getting there *too early*. The goal is for your child to make a strong association between peeing and his potty. The more often he uses his potty successfully, the better. Study his schedule carefully and make adjustments right away.

The eighteen month old is more mature. He is advancing rapidly and will naturally have other interesting things on his mind. Keeping his focus on the potty will not be as easy as it is with a younger baby. In the beginning, it's best not to interrupt a toddler who's deep in play. Wait for a natural pause and then take him to the potty.

After the first few weeks you can proceed much as you would with a younger baby. Allow your toddler to take a favorite toy (or anything else he chooses, except food) to the potty with him. It will give him the feeling of greater control and will help divert his attention should he begin to fidget.

At eighteen months, a child is at an in-between stage. Since some are a little more mature than others, I suggest you read Chapters Three *and* Four before you begin your child's training. You'll need ideas from both sections.

If you've already started training and are now having problems, simply stop all training for two weeks. Think about the steps you've taken, and how you've handled situations up to this point. See if you can figure out how things went wrong. If you've had problems, you're probably quite exasperated. Try to re-adjust your frame of mind, then begin again. I'm sure you'll dis-cover your errors. *Attitude is everything.*

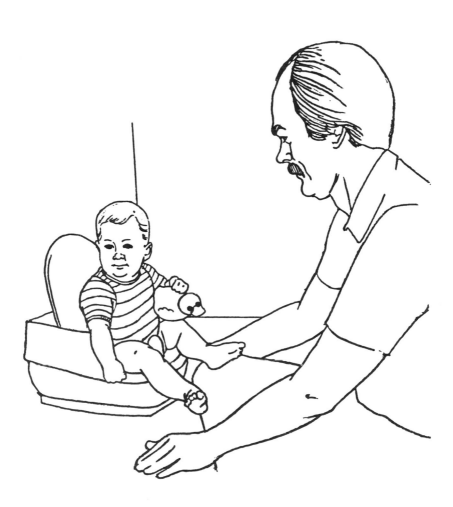

Child Sitting on Potty with Toy

4

The Two Year Old

Most people assume potty training consists of sitting their child on the potty and waiting until something happens, no matter how long it takes. They believe they should create a toilet schedule for their child and stick to it until he "learns," only to become exasperated and demanding when the child doesn't perform on command, or when accidents occur. This is definitely *not* the way to go about potty training.

A child must be allowed to make decisions about his own bodily functions. It is his right to do so. If you remove the sense of control from your child, you introduce a negative into the proceedings that is contrary to your best interests and to your child's. This is the most common mistake parents make. *They fail to respect the child's rights and individuality.*

Imagine for a moment how you'd feel if someone marched you onto the potty, time and again, and demanded that you pee or poop on command. Imagine what kind of attitude you'd develop toward the potty, your body and the person involved in your training. Yet, this is what many parents do.

If you scold or express disapproval because your child doesn't pee on command, you instill feelings of failure where failure simply does not exist. There is no failure on the potty. you either have to relieve yourself, or you don't. It's that simple. Once your child understands the process, he will take full responsibility for his toileting needs without your prompting.

Potty training progresses most quickly when a child is stimulated to want to use the toilet. This can't happen when emotional friction is being created by the parent. Training any child requires patience, respect and insight. If you don't show signs of disapproval, you let him know he's in control and that you aren't trying to force your will on something as personal as his own bodily functions. Toddlers have the same innate feelings about all this potty stuff as you do. If nobody dictates, no hang-ups are created.

NO! NO! NO!

As you begin your two year old's training, always keep in mind your child's growing need to display his independence. The best approach to take is one that works with—not against—the two year old's whims. At this age, the average toddler must almost always be given a reason to cooperate with the parent on any level.

Two year olds are contrarians. Tell the two year old it's time to eat and he'll say "no, not hungry." Tell him to pick up his toys and he'll just look at you. Tell him it's time to go and he'll dawdle. It seems that whenever parents tell the two year old what he must do, that becomes the one thing the child is least likely to *want* to do.

Obviously, this attitude cannot be allowed to flourish while training. Since certain parental approaches seem to trigger the toddler's negative response, it is imperative to keep to the path of least resistance.

Avoid Yes/No—Give Him Choices

Toddlers most often respond negatively when faced with yes/no situations. If you ask a two year old if he wants his shirt on, he'll often say no. But if you ask *which* shirt he wants to wear, the yellow or the blue, his mind shifts into another mode. He's being asked to make a decision. Decision-making allows him to affirm his independence. He enjoys this because it makes him feel powerful.

Since the toddler must constantly prove to himself that he has the right and the power to make choices, the opportunity to choose how or when to do something is important to him. Giving your child choices in potty training provides a solid network of activity that enables him to express himself. The feeling of control that is achieved provides substantial incentive to continue participating.

As training progresses, you should consistently provide new ways for your toddler to satisfy his need to assert himself and make choices. If you have more than one toilet, ask him which one he wants to pee in. Ask him, "Would you like to go outside after you pee?" With a little creativity on your part, you can come up with many ways of encouraging your toddler to use the potty, while avoiding the "yes, I will/no, I won't" situation.

A STRESS-FREE BEGINNING

Potty training should always be introduced as a fun activity. It should not be presented solely as a means of keeping the diaper dry or as a way of proving how grown-up your child can be.

Trying to pressure a child into wanting to use his potty is the most ineffective approach a parent can take. Pressure misdirects a child's focus. It creates internal stress and stirs up feelings of insecurity. As a result, the most common reaction to pressure is non-compliance, non-participation or tantrums. This can be avoided mostly by taking an easy-going attitude toward training. Getting a child into the mood to sit on a potty is easy if there are no pressures to overcome. It's even easier if using the potty is made to be fun. So why have it any other way?

MATERIAL REWARDS DON'T HELP

Some parents wrongly assume that rewarding a child with a new toy or trinket will persudade him to try harder to achieve bladder and bowel control. This just doesn't work. A child must be self-motivated to want to sit on a potty. Bribes teach a child how to manipulate; they do not motivate. *How* your toddler is made to feel about himself as he goes about his training, as well as *his perceptions of the task itself,* provides his greatest source of motivation.

SPARKING THE TWO YEAR OLD'S INTEREST

Take advantage of normal, everyday situations that tend to stimulate your two year old's curiosity. An obvious opportunity comes when your child follows you into the bathroom. Young children are intensely curious about bathroom behavior. Tots just can't resist tagging along when a parent goes to the toilet. Until now the toddler has only been a toilet spectator. Most aren't even allowed in the bathroom by themselves, which peaks their curiosity all the more.

Toddlers learn by imitating the actions of others. Ordinarily, they will watch their parents closely in order to better understand how something is done. Then they'll try doing it themselves. The fact that your child shows interest indicates a willingness to participate. When you are urinating and see your child watching you, ask if he'd like to try peeing on the toilet, too. If he says no, then respect his reply. But most often he will say "yes" because his urge to participate is so strong. Tell him that sitting on the potty is fun. As long as you're not trying to force him, it will be.

MAKING DECISIONS ABOUT THE POTTY

Ask your child if he'd like to have his own potty to pee in. Then take him with you to get a potty. Have fun shopping for it. In the store, let the child point to the ones he wants to try. Set them on the floor and let him look them over. See many different potties. Let him sit on them and ask if he likes each one. Observe the style your child is most attracted to. If he likes a type that might present problems, tell him you think it's nice, but "let's go look at some others in another store." Allow your child to have a choice, but don't let him select a potty you feel is wrong. Make sure the fit is right. When you bring the potty home, place it in the room where your child spends the most time.

FALSE CONTROL

By the second year, a toddler can be expected to go two or three hours without wetting. He may even stay dry throughout the night. His bladder no longer empties itself involuntarily. When the two year old wets, he pushes first. This is nature's way of indicating that bladder capacity is greater and the sphincter muscles have matured. It does *not* indicate that a toddler is purposely trying to control his bladder; nor does it imply that training will be easier or shorter in duration. It is important not to confuse what the body does naturally with what appears to be a child's command of his body. Your toddler still has much to learn about his body and controlling its functions. Full control comes only with practice and time.

HOW TO BEGIN TRAINING A TWO YEAR OLD

Every child is different, but each one develops a consistent daily pattern for wetting. Many wake up dry in the morning and after naps and will pee within a few minutes. Others will stay dry for an hour or more after waking. Watch your child throughout the day to determine his patterns. Begin sitting him on the potty a few times a day at approximately the time you'd expect him to wet. As you work with your child, you'll learn his patterns and be able to help him with great accuracy. This will enable him to more fully associate the process of removing the diaper, then sitting on the potty to pee. Be observant. Watch for clues that indicate it's time to go to the potty.

Don't assume that you can establish a new pattern for your child. This will only bring you frustration.

If you can't figure out when is the best time to go, wait about forty minutes after he's had something to drink, then see if he'll sit on the potty. Sit him there for no more than two or three minutes. As you wait, hold his attention by talking to him. You may want to give him some small object to play with. Make this a quiet time of gentle communication between the two of you.

Proper timing of urination becomes linked with the sensation felt when the diaper comes off. After a while, just removing the diaper will often stimulate the urge to pee. Let your toddler know that he can make himself pee when he wants. Make potty training fun. One way to do this is to joke about making pee-pee bubbles as urine hits the water in the toilet or bath. To the two year old, this is magic. He feels that he's making something special happen.

Use your imagination. You'll be surprised to learn how quickly your creativity will produce results. If your child enjoys making pee-pee bubbles for only a couple of weeks before losing interest, that's okay. During that time, he will have been making an extra effort toward control. That's the important point.

The toddler should be made to feel he's in charge as much as possible. If your child sees that you're having a good time, he's more likely to get into the spirit of it all. Your playful attitude is transferred to him. As a result, the training process goes more smoothly.

Don't Rush

During these first few weeks it's very important to go slowly. Keep diapers dry. Check your child often and change the diaper as soon as he wets or poops. A child who's allowed to stay in wet or poopy diapers becomes complacent to the feel of them. Keeping your child in dry diapers prevents this.

Talk to your toddler as you change him. Tell him he has wet or poopy diapers. Tell him this as a point of information—never with even a hint of disapproval.

As you do all this, you're acquainting your child with his body. In essence, you are helping to develop his whole attitude toward the potty, toilet training and his body. You want it to be a totally positive experience. So make it a fun, sharing experience.

Down and Out to Where?

Show your toddler how you empty the potty and encourage him to flush the toilet. If flushing seems to bother him, don't push.

Do it for him. Expect that your child will naturally want to know where his stuff is going. Be prepared to provide a simple explanation. I used to tell my son that his pee-pee was "going to be with all the other pee-pee." He thought that was okay and would happily say "bye-bye" to it each time the toilet was flushed. Use your imagination, but don't lie. Just make things as interesting as you can.

Avoid Pressure

Don't allow potty training to become a war of will. Potty training doesn't involve the teaching of discipline. *Never pressure your child for results.* If you do, you'll create an attitude problem. Imagine how you'd feel if someone dictated when and where you'd go next, hovering over you all the while, waiting. Toddlers are people, too! Alwqys treat your child with respect. Keep in mind that you're dealing with his self-esteem here. If he doesn't have to pee, then simply accept that. The gentler your attitude is, the better. If you show frustration or impatience, you may set training back months.

As you go about training, always take into consideration how the day is progressing for your child. If he's overly tired or fussy, skip sitting him on the potty at that time. Just change his diaper promptly when he wets. If family or guests are visiting, and the normal routine of the house is disrupted, then relax training for the day if it seems to create any friction. Some children just don't want to do it when other people are around.

Stepping Things Up

After a week or so, when your child has become accustomed to sitting on the potty, begin placing him on it as soon as he wakes up in the morning and right after nap time. Limit sitting on the potty to four or five times a day.

Because the two year old's state of mind is so set on the idea of staying in charge, it is imperative that you not push. Encourage him, but don't let your good intentions develop into a negative situation. Remember that a toddler will not necessarily need to pee simply because you are placing him on his potty. Whenever your child shows resistance, skip that time to sit.

Within a few months your toddler will have it all figured out. Sitting on the potty will become an easy, familiar task. The toddler will establish his own schedule. *He* will tell *you* when he has a wet diaper.

Some children will come to you as soon as they wet so they may be changed immediately. Others might wiggle out of their diaper, taking care of the problem on their own.

Since timing may not be accurate for most children at this point, getting to the potty on their own before wetting begins can sometimes be a problem. Don't be surprised if the toddler tells you he has to pee as he is doing so.

Help your child onto his potty immediately whenever he exhibits a need during the day. Often, he may get onto the potty and find that nothing happens. Be just as supportive when he doesn't wet as you are when he does. Never discourage a child's efforts to master all this. Always show him that you are there for him. This encourages him to communicate with you all the more.

On To Training Pants

Once your child is regularly letting you know it's time to pee, you should begin to gradually move from diapers to training pants. There are several types of panties your child can wear. Four- and five-ply are best. Avoid terrycloth panties until your child has reduced his number of accidents to a minimum, because they provide the least absorbency.

Make sure the panties you buy are big enough for your child to easily pull down by himself. You don't want your child to become frustrated because his panties are stuck! Pay particular attention to the leg openings. There should be enough elastic for ample stretch. If possible, try a pair on your child to be sure. This is one area where being a "size two" might mean wearing a "size four" panty.

A Big Change

Toddlers really do enjoy wearing training pants. They are much more comfortable than diapers. Everything about them feels quite different. Wearing a panty can be very symbolic, as it seems to prove to the toddler that he is now a "big kid."

It's not unusual for a toddler to begin to react differently to situations once the panty goes on with regularity. Expect to see a surge of independent behavior. Instead of the toddler allowing you to help him into the car, he might demand the right to get in by himself. Or he may want to wash himself without your assistance. As these situations occur, it's important for you to step back and encourage your child's independent behavior.

The Beginning Of The End

Once your child has developed enough confidence in himself, he will gradually begin to assume more responsibility for his actions. The toddler will eventually decide that he doesn't require his parents' assistance to sit on the potty. Instead, he'll decide to do it on his own. This is a very big step for the toddler to make and his efforts should not be underrated.

A two year old can get out of panties long before he can get back into them, so you may sometimes find your child playing bare-bottomed. Upon inspection you'll find that the potty has been used without your knowing it. And sometimes your child will call you to the potty to see he's done it all by himself. Make a big deal out of this. Show your child how happy and proud you are of him.

Toddlers love having the upper hand. Having the power to control his functions successfully, without parental assistance, is an all-time high. This quickly becomes a powerful incentive, reaffirming his independence. However, there will be some inconsistency in his control and potty use. Your child will still need your loving guidance to remind him that it's potty time.

When your toddler consistently lets you know when he needs to get on the potty and "accidents" seldom occur, you can start using training pants exclusively (except when the child is sleeping). You may want to use a plastic panty over the training pants for extra peace of mind.

When your child has used the potty alone several times in a row, stop taking him to his potty unless he comes to you for help or begins to have some accidents. If your child begins to have more than a few accidents, then take control of the situation again and go back to helping him to the potty for a while. *Do not revert back to diapers.* When he begins to assert himself once again, allow him to continue on his own.

Let him take it on his own for as long as he can. Expect some accidents, though. It's not uncommon for a child to come get you in order to show you where he made a puddle. When this happens, explain that it was an accident. Talk about it, but don't lose your cool. Tell him he's not supposed to pee on the floor or furniture. Let him watch as you clean it up and repeat again, calmly, that pee doesn't go here—it goes in the potty.

Help him into a clean pair of pants after you clean up the mess. Then, don't refer to the accident again. Move ahead and don't let it become an issue.

Soon your toddler will complete his training on his own. But you'll still need to help out with wiping and getting pants up, and with occasional reminders.

THE TWO AND A HALF YEAR OLD

Developmentally, the two and a half year old has progressed a great deal and has matured considerably. He can feed himself and do all sorts of things. He is more self-assured than he was just a few months earlier. Physically, the older toddler is capable of full control of his bladder and bowel. He can also communicate his needs more clearly. In many ways he has become a very independent little person.

The two and a half year old toddler is certainly becoming aware of the inconveniences of wearing a diaper. Most have reached a point where they are unable to tolerate the feel of a wet one. It may even embarrass them. It's at this point that a child, even without any adult assistance, would begin to potty train himself. Being in diapers is a very delicate issue at this age, and should be treated as such. Be considerate as you begin to potty train a child of this age.

The older toddler's increased intellectual development is definitely an asset to potty training. However, he can hardly be considered mature, so keep in mind that you are still dealing with a very young mind. Never try to shame your child because he is still in diapers. If he's in diapers at this age, it's because you haven't helped him to get out of them. No child should be ridiculed because of that.

To begin training a two and a half year old, follow the guidelines in the two year old training section and adapt the ideas to fit the needs of your child. Keep in mind that there will be subtle differences between the ages. Not only is the two and a half year old more mature, he is physically larger. As a result, your child may or may not need to have a potty of his own to use. If he's big enough to be using an adult toilet, then let him. Or get a simple potty top for him to use. But if your child seems the least bit uncomfortable sitting up on a regular toilet, get him a potty.

Don't expect overnight results even though you're dealing with an older child. Like the younger child, he must learn things about his body. The greatest part of his training will be spent practicing the art of control. Depending upon the child, training may take anywhere from one to five or six months to complete.

5

Bowel Training

A good working relationship with one's bowel is one of the most important factors associated with a long and healthy life. Bowel movements should come freely and easily, and with the body's own natural rhythms. Today, adults everywhere fight a daily battle with constipation and hemorrhoids as a direct result of situations they encountered as children during potty training. Certainly our diet has much to do with the situation. But inadequate, stressful bowel training has at least as much to do with it. This is an unfortunate situation and something you can help your child to avoid.

There's often more stress associated with bowel training than with anything else a young child encounters. Because it smells and is messy, bowel movements often irritate the adults in the child's life who have to deal with cleaning it up. Yet the movement is very personal to the child. It is a part of his being. The child may feel that if adults think there's something wrong with his bowel movement, then there must be something wrong with him personally. Consider it from his point of view and past experience. Most everything he does is great. When he starts to crawl, it's wonderful. When he starts to walk, it's terrific. When he tries to feed himself and makes a big mess, his parents are often amused and offer encouragement. But when he poops, the atmosphere suddenly changes. Things aren't so wonderful anymore. The adults are irritated and he knows he's the cause of it.

The adult who displays frustration, annoyance or intolerance toward the child's bowel movement sends mixed and confusing signals to the child. If a child has to contend with such narrow-mindedness, his relationship with and control of this natural function can easily become abnormal. This is quite disruptive to the bowel training process.

The elimination of waste is an entirely normal and healthy process. Babies don't have any negative feelings about bowel movements or bowel training until *you* create them. When a child is given the opportunity to learn about his body and its functions without pressure, potty training progresses more rapidly.

Bowel training should be conducted within an atmosphere of approval and acceptance. The experiences the child has during training will lay the foundation for his personal attitudes, and will be with him all his life. How you react, what you say, the impressions you give—all have a direct influence on how the child will come to feel about himself and his bowel functions.

HOW BOWEL MOVEMENTS OCCUR

Throughout the day, wave-like movements propel waste material through the bowel. The encircling muscles contract to squeeze waste material forward. Sometimes intestinal activity is strongly felt, causing a cramping sensation—especially early in the day. At other times, only a vague sensation occurs. Any bowel activity that is strong enough to be felt is a signal that a movement is possible. Obviously, you become aware of bowel activity when you feel cramping in that area. But recognizing the more subtle activity enables a person to have a movement at a time that might otherwise have been missed.

It's not necessary to have strong intestinal contractions in order to produce a bowel movement. Therefore, it's important for a child to be given the opportunity to recognize the more subtle activity prior to his movements. As he grows older, familiarity with his body's inner working will enable him to control his bowel easily, instead of having *it* control *him* by failing to work when he wants it to.

BOWEL TRAINING

Bowel training requires a special sense of communication with your child. It also requires that you not pressure him and that you and the other adults in his life not display an aversion toward his movements or disdain in cleaning him afterwards. Similar to bladder training, progress comes in stages. It doesn't happen overnight.

This bowel training program is divided into three steps and can begin at approximately fifteen months of age. The first two steps involve helping the child to recognize bowel sensations, then to connect those sensations to bowel movements. These first steps take only a few months to complete and do not involve actually sitting on a potty. Once your child has gained an awareness of these processes, he will be better able to actively participate in bowel training. As he gains independence, he will naturally assume more and more responsibility for his bowel movements. Depending upon the child, training may be completed before the second birthday.

Step 1. The first step is helping your child to recognize that he is having a movement. No matter what the child's age, you begin training by simply pointing out that he is having a bowel movement. It doesn't matter one bit if he is on his potty at the time or pooping in his diaper. You simply want him to start to recognize sensations. Attempts toward actual control will come later. Making him aware of his body as it is functioning is the important thing right now. If your child is clearly aware of his bowel movements as they are occurring, then move on to Step 2 at the very beginning of bowel training.

As you begin training, bring it to your child's attention whenever he passes gas. This is simply to focus his attention on another function of his body's workings. However, a whiff of gas or a bowel movement shouldn't be made a negative issue. Hard as it sometimes is, never imply to your child that whatever he has done smells bad or causes you displeasure. No holding the nose or "peeeeyewww." It might make your baby feel that something is wrong with him, causing him to become embarrassed or ashamed. Everything you say or do is part of your baby's educational process. He may pick up on even the slightest things.

Since children do not generally have bowel movements when they're on the go, catching them in the act is usually not difficult. If you watch your child closely you'll notice that he will usually become quite still prior to and during bowel movements. His breathing will deepen and become rhythmic. After a minute or two it will be all over. Tell your child what's happening as he is having a movement.

Show him the contents of his diaper afterward. Seeing what his body produces allows a toddler to connect the sensations with the final product. It also makes his movements seem more real, because they are no longer just a feeling to him, but something he can actually *see*. Before this point, the toddler is somewhat disconnected from the process because he hasn't made this basic connection. When showing him his movements, a statement like "Hey, look what you just did" is enough. There's no need to make a big production out of it.

As you observe your child, take notice of when his movements normally occur. The majority will have bowel movements in the morning. After a nighttime of inactivity, the colon is easily stimulated by the morning meal.

However, if there happens to be a lot of excitement in your home or circumstances require a change in his daily routine, it's not unusual for him to delay his functions until a quieter time comes along. Children are very much like adults in this respect.

Of course, children have bowel movements at all hours of the day—not just in the morning. Every child has different habits, and a young one's regularity often fluctuates. Don't expect to catch him in the act every time—just do what you can and be relaxed about it. He'll soon understand. Once you feel that your child is always aware of when he is having a bowel movement, it's time to move on to the next step.

Step 2. The second step involves teaching your child to recognize the sensations of bowel activity prior to having a movement.

A child doesn't feel the exact same level of intestinal activity prior to all movements. Intensity varies. By bringing his attention to the inner process, he becomes attuned to these variations. This will become an asset in later training. By then he will be more apt to notice preliminary bowel activity in time to take control of the situation.

By this time, you should be quite familiar with your child's habits and his body's actions both before and during his movements. As soon as you notice the preliminaries, ask him if he's about to have a bowel movement. (Use your own special words for it; do-do, poopy, etc.) He will soon come to recognize the early sensations associated with the process.

Many parents believe that the prime objective of bowel training is to keep the child from messing in his pants. Of course that's part of it, but keep in mind that a child is not a child forever. If a toddler fails to learn how to recognize his body's signals, he will eventually become an adult with the same problem. Thus, constipation could plague him all his life.

If a person hasn't learned to recognize the more subtle range of activity that his body produces, he will miss opportunities to have an easy, convenient bowel movement. Instead, he will tighten his anus until the sensation passes. Then, sometime later, the bowel will begin the process again. Only this time it won't be ignored and the child will be subject to the pain of cramps and/or large stools. This can create a vicious cycle in childhood, where the child holds back a movement for fear of pain, eventually leading to constipation.

Step 3. The third step involves developing the ability to consciously control the bowel. This enables the toddler to delay a movement until he can get to a potty.

After you've spent a few months helping your child to focus on how his bowel feels prior to and during a movement, you can start to place him on his potty for bowel movements. Most children will be very comfortable with their potties by this time, since bladder training will have begun much earlier.

Begin by gently introducing the idea of pooping in the potty instead of in the diaper. Watch him closely at the time of day when his movements most often occur. When you observe his preliminary signals, sit him on the potty. Tell him that you'd like him to try to have a movement there, using the familiar words

Child at Play on Potty

you use to describe it. A child of this age will usually be able to clearly indicate "yes" or "no." If he says yes, smile and be quiet with him. If he says no, don't force him to sit on the potty any longer.

If you have problems getting your child to sit on the potty long enough to complete the job, find something interesting for him to do which will hold his attention. Books are a good choice. I bought my son some magnetic letters which he could stick on the side of the refrigerator in the kitchen, next to the potty. He'd tell me which word he wanted to spell and I'd tell him what letters to get. It was fun and made sitting on the potty easier for him.

Don't assume that you know best about when your child needs to have a movement and never rush your child once he is sitting on the potty. If you try to direct the toddler's bowel movements, he will become confused and frustrated. Expecting him to produce a bowel movement just because you'd like him to is not only unrealistic, it's unreasonable. Until now, your child's movements have been free and natural. There's no reason to expect this to change.

At first, placing your child on his potty for pooping may be confusing to him. Since the potty has only been used to pee in up to this point, your child will have to make some mental adjustments. Altering his habit of pooping in his diaper takes a while. As long as you're not dictating and making him feel like this is a "must do" situation, he should find the idea interesting. He already knows quite a bit about his body and how it works— now he just needs to put it all together.

The "Poop In The Potty" Panic

It isn't uncommon for a toddler to go into a near panic the first few times he uses the potty or the toilet for bowel movements. When a child experiences something new and unfamiliar, some anxiety can be expected. Having his movements go into a potty feels so different that he may easily become unsure or frightened. I remember my son having a fit the first few times he sat on the potty. Now, it's an event! He really enjoys himself.

Don't let your child's reaction cause you to panic. Reassure your child and do whatever you can to shift his attention. Empty the potty immediately. Clean it and flush the toilet. Talk to your child the whole time, explaining what has happened and what you are doing for him.

Don't dismiss or make light of your child's fear. This is a real concern. Let him know that you understand, but that things are really okay. To a great degree, your compassionate response will determine how long such a fear may last.

Dealing With Accidents

It's important to encourage a child to respond to his body signals. Trust him. Expect that he will do just fine and, in time, he will. Don't worry if your child has accidents. You should expect them. When they do occur, be sure to avoid the use of negative phrasing. Avoid the "not" words: can't, won't, don't. Stay away from phrases like "Why can't you do this right?" or "You're not trying." Negatives only serve to tear down a child's self-esteem, leaving him with a feeling of incompetence. Obviously, this has no place in training.

When you deal with accidents, use only positive reinforcements as you talk to your child. Say things like "Soon you'll do it in the potty all the time" and "Things like this happen sometimes because you're still learning." Find ways to let your child know that you have confidence in him and his abilities to grow and progress.

Timing

Most toddlers don't have a clear concept of time, so getting to a potty in time will be a problem in the beginning. Often, a toddler will come to you just as his movement is beginning. If you can, get him to his potty even if it's already begun. He's trying, and it's up to you to encourage his efforts. If you decide not to take him to the potty just because the movement is already in progress, you may give him the message that poor timing is reason enough to quit trying. His efforts to alert you will seem un-important. This can be an emotional letdown for the toddler.

Whenever a child thinks he needs to go (even when you don't), he should be encouraged to try. If he does have a movement, praise him. If he does nothing at all, let him know that's fine, too. He's trying, and that's all that matters.

Be Calm and Supportive

Early on, a toddler tends to overreact to his body's signals. He wants to keep his diapers clean, so he's constantly on the look-out for his next bowel movement. It's not unusual for him to confuse passing gas with a coming movement. To him, gas may feel like the beginning of a bowel movement and he won't be sure he can fully control it. This may cause a near panic as he insists upon getting to the potty immediately. Don't try to sec-ond-guess the situation. Put him on the potty immediately. This won't happen often, but it will happen. As soon as he's had some success getting to the potty in time, he'll develop enough confidence in his capabilities.

Don't increase his frustration by becoming frustrated your-self. He needs your understanding and encouragement.

Keep in mind that, once a child is on the potty, it will proba-bly take a few minutes before his bowel will move. Be patient. Don't keep referring to his bowel or what you expect of him. He doesn't have to be reminded again and again what he is there to do. A parent who repeatedly prods a child creates pressure where none should exist. This pressure causes the child's atten-tion to shift from his body to the emotional pressure that the parent is presenting. The more the parent pushes, the less atten-tion a child is able to direct toward the actual process at hand.

I don't know of a single person who could have a bowel move-ment with someone pushing them to do so. There's no reason why a child should be expected to react any differently. Be con-siderate. Be patient. Good training allows a child to progress at his own speed. Learning to respond to one's bowel and get to a potty takes time and practice. Some children will acquire this ability within a few months; others will take more time. But all children eventually master the process.

Encourage Participation

Some toddlers have no problem producing a bowel movement when placed on a potty. Others require some incentive. For example, my son had a real fascination with his "wet wipes" and constantly wanted to get into them. I started letting him have one every time he sat down on the potty to poop. He could use this to wipe himself, too. Even though his "wipe" was more of a pat, it became a part of his own ritual. See what works with your child.

Allow your toddler to assume control at whatever time he chooses. As long as he is gently encouraged to participate in his own potty training, he won't develop negative attitudes toward it. As he enters into a certain stage of independent thinking, assuming total control over his body will become an easy step to take. You cannot push him into taking control before he's ready. Pressuring him will only slow down the process.

Once your child has gotten used to having bowel movements in his potty, he will automatically enter into the final phase of training. He will begin going to the potty to poop all by himself! When this begins, let him make a go of it on his own. If he begins to have accidents, try helping him onto the potty for a few more weeks. Soon he will be taking responsibility for his own movements *without* your help.

Due to the toddler's growing sense of independence, it's not unusual for a child who has been using the potty regularly to suddenly regress and begin messing his diapers once again. This has more to do with his state of mind than with bowel training. Don't become frustrated and make an issue out of this. Instead, be patient. "This, too, shall pass." Nobody really likes sitting in poop.

Cleaning Up

The young toddler faces two obstacles that prevent him from properly cleaning himself after bowel movements. His arms are too short to reach the anal area, and he lacks the necessary level of dexterity. So until your child is about two and a half years old, you're going to have to do his final wiping for him. Most children will insist on participating in the clean-up. Although your child won't be able to clean himself well, let him try anyway before you finish the job for him.

As you begin to teach your child to use toilet paper, encourage him to wipe first, then go over the area yourself to insure a proper job. Always explain to your child that both of you are cleaning his bottom to get all the poop off!

Because the toddler has a problem getting to that area, many will try reaching between their legs and wiping from back to front. Girls, especially, should be discouraged from this practice because of the increased risk of infection. Carefully explain that wiping should be done from *front to back.*

Once your child is physically capable of reaching the area, he should begin taking some responsibility for cleaning himself. If your child balks at cleaning himself, explain that everybody has to wipe—even Mommies and Daddies. Encourage him with a positive attitude toward his accomplishments. He will soon forget that he ever objected to the idea! Don't allow a child to manipulate you to keep doing this job for him. There really *does* come a time when helping your child actually becomes counterproductive.

CONSTIPATION AND DIET

Parents often make the assumption that, unless their child has a daily bowel movement, then he must be constipated. This is not true. Constipation is determined by the consistency of a stool, not the frequency of movements. For some children, a bowel movement every two days could be considered normal.

The chief causes of constipation are dairy products and foods low in roughage, breads, potatoes, rice cereal, applesauce, bananas, and macaroni, to name a few. Because these foods hold very little moisture, their residue tends to be dry or packed by the time it reaches the rectum.

Babies who consume whole or homogenized milk are often constipated, since stomach acid produces a large curd when it comes in contact with cow's milk. This curd quickly becomes hard and dry, producing a potential constipating agent. Babies who are breast-fed do not have this problem unless their system is sabotaged by junk foods and the lack of a balanced diet. This is because mother's milk is digested almost 100% by babies.

If your child is having a problem with constipation or hard stools, do not give him a laxative without a doctor's specific instructions. Instead, cut down on constipating foods and add bulk and fiber to his diet, along with plenty of liquids. Avoid wheat cereals, as wheat often causes reactions, cramps, gas or diarrhea. Give him fruits (other than bananas) and fruit juices each day.

Don't expect water to soften the stools. Water does little to counteract constipation because it isn't absorbed into the intestines in the same way fruits and vegetable juices are. Water gets directed toward the kidneys.

When a laxative is needed, use a natural one. Barley and oats produce a mild laxative effect. Prune juice offers a strong effect. If you use prune juice, do so in small amounts because diarrhea can result. If constipation continues to be a problem, contact your doctor for further instruction.

TEARS AND FEARS

If your child experiences a painful movement, it's possible that a hard stool created a tear at the anal opening. This is called an anal fissure and will naturally cause the next movement to hurt, as well. If this has occurred, a little Vaseline will help ease the problem. Dab a little on the area after each movement. Do this for a day or two.

Sometimes, tears are the result of a too vigorous rubbing with dry toilet paper. This scratches the skin, allowing bacteria to flourish. Inflammation follows. Adding a few drops of water to the toilet paper provides a more efficient clean-up and avoids the abrasive effects of dry paper.

Emotional or physical tension will also tighten the sphincter muscle. Babies who fear having a movement often constipate themselves simply by holding back. If your toddler seems to be afraid of a bowel movement, quietly distract him while he's on the potty. Sing a song, look at a picture book, or give him a special toy to play with. He'll still be aware of what he's doing, but won't be focusing his *entire* attention on his actions. Point out what he has done after the movement is finished. Show enthusiasm. Be calmly reassuring. In this way, after a few successful movements, you'll have helped him past his fear.

And remember—don't put a fearful child on an adult toilet. When his stool splashes into the toilet water, it could make him all the more frightened.

THE BIG NO-NO

As horrible as it may seem, it's quite possible to one day find your own sweet child smearing his bowel movement all over the place and having a wonderful time as he does so. This could make you crazy, but don't let it throw you off balance. Small children have absolutely no objection to the sight, smell or feel of their own stool. Once they get their hands on it, the urge to smoosh it between fingers and toes or to finger paint with it becomes almost irresistible.

If this happens with your child, above all, try to remain calm. How you react, what you say and how you say it will be remembered for a long time. Treat the situation calmly, as you would any other. Let your child know that playing in poop is a no-no. As you clean up the mess, firmly explain that poop goes in the diaper or in the potty, *not* in his hair or on the bars of his crib. Let him know that you really dislike what he's done, but keep in mind his immaturity and total innocence. Don't belittle him. Just clean up the mess and keep your fingers crossed that it won't happen again. Most likely, it won't.

6

Thoughts For All Ages

Every child goes through potty training in his own unique way. So does every parent. Because circumstances vary in each home, there may be situations which affect the training process that will require your special attention. Divorce, illness, a new baby are all obvious distractions to the toddler being trained because high levels of family stress are involved. So is teasing or a family member refusing to participate in the child's training. This chapter contains suggestions for the parent who encounters such problems. It also has some thoughts for the working parent.

AVOID ANY AND ALL NEGATIVES

Potty training your baby is a family affair. Everyone in your family should be made aware of the do's and don'ts of training. A father's role is especially important. Men often brag about their refusal to change a diaper or to participate in any way in the training. This is ridiculous. It doesn't add to the masculine image at all. *And it's bad for your baby.*

A baby develops his sense of importance and self-esteem through his parents' eyes. Their attitudes tell him that he's loved, accepted and has a place in the world. A child is naturally going to become suspicious upon hearing Dad proclaim that diapering or potty training is something he's not going to do.

Babies understand things intuitively. Don't underestimate their little minds just because they can't talk. If Dad (or anyone else) complains or shows displeasure about the baby's natural

Dad's Involvement in the Toilet Training Process

functions, your child will quickly get the idea that something about his body is bad. This immediately creates a very negative self-impression in a child. Not only does this make training more difficult, it can give your child a psychological scar he'll carry with him for the rest of his life. This is such an unfortunate problem. If this is an issue in your home, try to overcome it for the sake of your child. Tell Dad (and anyone else who acts in this way) to grow up!

TEASING

Teasing is a part of life. It's one of the ways we have fun with each other. But we must be very careful when it comes to teasing young children. You may say something playfully which a child will take very seriously. Comments about smelly diapers, poop, genitals or anything else associated with elimination or potty training may imply criticism. Such teasing can drastically affect your child's self-image.

From the time a child's first diaper is changed, he is subjected to comments about the contents. Parents think nothing of making a big deal out of a smelly diaper in front of their babies. And if anyone else is in the room, there may be jokes, further discussion and turned-up noses. Just because a baby can't understand words yet doesn't mean impressions aren't made. They are.

A lot of teasing centers around gas. Adults seldom make comments to other adults when they pass wind. But few adults seem able to resist teasing a child about it. Acting startled, smiling, and asking "Did you poot?" isn't critical teasing. But saying something like "Oh, wow, who stunk up the room?" and making a big issue out of it can have a lasting negative impression.

Babies absorb this kind of thing like a sponge. They don't reason out a teasing person's motive. They take most things at face value. To a child, comments of a personal nature are truthful statements. He may not get the joke. If a child's response to teasing appears to be one of embarrassment and discomfort, he may believe that a critical judgment has been made about him. He could begin to feel that something might be wrong with him.

Many parents fail to understand how teasing can create such an impression because they fail to see the situation in full. Adults have the capacity to reason; babies do not. It's that simple. Children learn to judge themselves through the actions and reactions of others. What they see and hear in their own home carries great weight.

If you really can't resist the urge to tease, then *make sure your child understands that you are playing*. And please don't be critical or run it into the ground. Don't embarrass or shame your child. If you make a joke that results in a confused look on the child's face, then stop. Take the time to reassure him that all is well, that you love him, and that you were only playing.

A SPECIAL CONSIDERATION

At about the same time toddlers are being potty trained, they are also rediscovering their genitals. This is normal and important behavior. A child must become completely familiar with all his body parts. If a parent starts slapping hands, or telling the child that touching there is wrong, the toddler will make negative connections between his genitals, himself and potty training. He may come to believe he's "dirty" in some way. This can drastically lower a child's self-esteem.

A toddler simply doesn't comprehend any so-called differences between his ears, nose, toes or genitals. They are all *him*. It makes no sense to a child why he can play with his toes but not with his genitals. Boys may have an especially hard time because they routinely touch their penis when peeing. They fail to see any logic in why they aren't supposed to touch it at any other time.

Don't misdirect a child's focus by bringing such a negative element to his attention. Your child's need to constantly touch himself will pass. But impressions you give him about his genitals will not.

WHAT!? NO POTTY!?

During the course of training, you should let your child go to the bathroom somewhere other than on the potty. This experience should be offered *before* your child's toileting ideas become too set. It has been every parent's experience that as soon as you're about as far from a bathroom as you can get, your child will have to go.

Many parents let their children use the great outdoors in the summertime. Sometimes, you might even let your child pee in a cup or pail. It may sound silly to encourage this, but there will come a time when there won't be a restroom available. Or he'll be asked for a urine specimen at the doctor's office. If your child is firmly fixed on the toilet being the *only* place to go, it could cause some unnecessary stress. Many adults find it impossible to relieve themselves anywhere other than in the toilet, no matter how hard they try. This is the direct result of fixations they developed in childhood.

This is one thing I forgot to consider in my daughter's training. As a result it really caused her problems. The first time I noticed it, we were driving through Arkansas. It was about midnight, we were out in the middle of nowhere in a heavy thunderstorm, and Tiffany announced that she had to pee. She was twenty-five months old at the time and had been completely potty trained for quite some time, so there was no way she was going to wet her pants. At first I told her she was going to have to wait because there was no restroom around. Within minutes she started fussing and telling us that she had to go right then and there.

Since we had nowhere to stop in the heavy downpour, I found a cup for her to use. I will never forget the look of horror on her face when I presented her with that cup to pee in. She thought that I had completely lost my mind. After all, you *drink* from cups, and as far as she was concerned that was *all* you did with them. She sat back down and stared at me in utter disbelief as her father and I tried to convince her it was all right to use a cup in an emergency like this. We told her stories about how we did precisely the same thing and that it was okay to do so. But she was adamant in her refusal to participate in something as offensive as that. The poor child held it in for another hour before relief finally came. With all of that rain, it must have been the longest hour she ever spent. Now, even as a young adult, she still can't bring herself to pee in a cup.

BENEFITS OF SUMMER

Summer is especially wonderful when you're a toddler. After being indoors for most of the winter, going out and getting dirty can be a fine time, indeed. Once outside, most toddlers just don't want to go back into the house for any reason—not even to sit on the potty. So many parents allow their babies to pee outside.

Kids like to pee outdoors. It's great fun and a much enjoyed change of pace. Since it is so much fun, toddlers pay close atten-

The Great Outdoors

tion to what they're doing as they do it. This focused awareness is excellent practice and has its own special reward for the child.

Not only do children like doing it while they're outside, *they also like to go outside just to do it.* If your child is playing inside and tells you he needs to pee, take advantage of the situation. Ask him if he wants to pee outside instead. Most children will be delighted with the opportunity.

It doesn't take long for a child to realize that, by wetting his diaper, he misses the chance to go in the grass or to watch it fall on the sand or ground. Once the idea sticks, most toddlers somehow manage to control their bladders more efficiently in order to get the privilege of going outside.

Some children enjoy peeing on the ground so much that as soon as they dribble a few drops, they may run to another spot and try to do some more. Boys, especially, find this a fun thing to do, probably because it gives even the shortest toddler the freedom to stand and pee unaided. Outings such as this give a child more practice and often become a nice incentive to keep dry. Before long, what started out as a fun thing provides a very interesting way to complete bladder training.

USING THE BIG POTTY

Toddlers are a lot of fun once they begin using the big toilet. They insist on trying out every possible position: facing the back of the toilet, squatting, sitting sideways. Some will even stand on the rim of the toilet. Boys are obviously the best equipped to pull this one off, but girls will try it, too. Kids love trying new positions. And there's no reason to discourage this. As long as what's coming out goes into the right spot, why make a fuss?

STANDING UP

Boys generally begin bladder training sitting down. After a while their desire to imitate Dad or other boys motivates them to stand. It's not unusual for a toddler as young as sixteen months to want to stand up to pee. At this age, he might suddenly stand up on the rim of the toilet seat to go. Or, without thinking of the consequences, he might stand in front of the toilet and pee on the floor.

Standing on the seat works amazingly well for some little boys. But if your child's aim is off, don't discourage him. Some children have a tendency to overshoot the toilet if they're standing on the seat, so be prepared to get him a stool or step ladder.

Facing the Back of the Toilet

Find something that will provide enough height for him to reach over the rim of the toilet.

There's really no set time when boys begin standing while peeing. Some try early, some wait a while. If your son shows no interest in it, then don't push. Sooner or later, he will.

Standing on Rim of Toilet Seat

THE CHILD SAYS NO

Sometimes a child will suddenly balk at the idea of sitting on the potty and might even go so far as to not want his diaper changed. Not to worry—this is only a passing problem. New stimulation may have caused a temporary shift in attitude. This could be the result of a recent illness. It could be that teething is causing the baby pain and frustration. If a baby isn't feeling well, he just might not want to be bothered. Let him rest and don't push him to use the potty. Being off the potty for a few days shouldn't cause him to regress from the progress that he's already made. Always be sensitive to his frustrations and try not to magnify them by forcing the issue. He'll be back to normal before you know it.

A child might also protest sitting on his potty because he wants to imitate Mom and Dad and go on the big toilet. Give it a try. If you have a potty top that fits on the big toilet, sit him up there. If you don't have one, either hold him on the toilet and support him with your hands or have him sit facing the back of the toilet. If your child likes it, encourage him to use the big toilet whenever he wants. More than likely, your child will use both the potty *and* the toilet once he realizes that he has a choice in the matter.

CAN'T FEEL THE WET

If you're using super-absorbent disposable diapers, there's something you must consider. In the beginning of potty training, it's important for a child to learn the feeling of "wet." If the diaper prevents that sensation, then you're going to have a problem. A baby must recognize the difference between wet and dry. The primary reason for changing a dirty diaper immediately is to allow these comparisons to be made. You want your child to recognize that he is wet as soon as he possibly can. For this reason alone, these diapers are not recommended.

THE RUNAWAY

At some point, all babies will run from their parents when told it's time for a diaper change or time to sit on the potty. Many experts believe that this indicates the child isn't ready for training. They even go so far as to say that the child prefers a dirty diaper and is possessive about its contents. But this line of reasoning is short-sighted. A baby who runs away or refuses to be placed on the potty is simply expressing a sense of independence. This is perfectly normal behavior and shouldn't be treated as anything less. It's not "wrong," and it's not rebellious. This type of behavior occurs in various forms throughout a child's life, but for some reason is often singled out as some kind of warning signal when associated with potty training.

Children between the ages of one and two are just beginning to gain some independence. They'll run just as quickly when their parent says it's time for a bath or a nap. So recognize the situation for what it is. Keep your wits about you and never stifle a child who's trying to assert himself in this manner. This simply means that your baby is shifting into a new phase of development.

Instead of fighting with your child about his running away, give him a little more responsibility in the routine. Perhaps you can have him go get a clean diaper when a change is needed. Or you might let him dispose of the wet one after the change. Allow him to have more participation and stimulate his sense of accomplishment.

THE BLADDER REVOLT

One of the more common situations which occurs during training is when a child wets his pants as he pitches a fit. When this happens to a child who's nearly trained, it's easy for a parent to conclude that their child is wetting his pants on purpose. Often, the situation is made worse by scolding or spanking as punishment for this "revolt."

You must always remember that your child is still learning to control his body. Such wetting as this is involuntary. When a child throws a temper tantrum, he releases a tremendous amount of energy. In effect, his little system overloads and he loses control of his bladder.

If you react to the wetting with anger, you'll only make the situation worse. Not only will your child have experienced an emotional upset, but he will be punished for something he couldn't control. This creates tremendous feelings of failure and shame. Accidents will then become more frequent because the child's subconscious retains those feelings of inadequacy.

If your child wets his pants when he's upset, don't make an issue out of it. Handle the situation as calmly as you can and help him into dry panties. Let this be as natural as wiping away his tears and runny nose. As your child gains emotional maturity, this type of accident will cease to occur.

THE FINAL FRONTIER

As a child reaches the final stages of training, the ability to control his sphincter muscles increases. He realizes that he is becoming the master of his bladder and will want to discover just how far his control can go. He will try to hold back peeing as long as he possibly can.

He's testing his limits, and sometimes he'll wait just a little *too* long. You may see him walking with his knees together or holding his hand between his legs. You'll ask him if he has to pee. He'll say "no." This is a natural situation and you should gently encourage him to stop what he's doing and take time to empty his bladder.

Be playful about it, rather than dictatorial. If you know he needs to go but he says "no," don't acknowledge the no. Act as if you didn't hear it. Quickly try to focus his attention on the potty. Say something like, "Oh-oh, where's your potty? Let's get there quickly. I'll bet I can get there before you do." Or if you're outside, you may say something like, "Oh, look at this little pile of sand. Come here and pee on it." Whatever strikes your fancy will probably work fine.

WASHING HANDS

Many parents go overboard when it comes to washing hands. They insist that their child wash every time they use the potty because they relate it to proper bathroom etiquette. Requiring a child to wash after using the bathroom is certainly in order if they've gotten something on their hands. But many parents require their child to wash no matter what.

"You wash when you're dirty." That's what children are taught. If they have to wash simply because they've touched their privates, it may tell them that their private parts are dirty in some mysterious way. That is unhealthy. It leads to a negative self-image.

When your child gets off the potty, ask "Did you get any pee or poop on your hands?" If he did, you can bet he'll find it. If something is on his hands, help him wash. Otherwise, don't insist on an unnecessary ritual.

WHEN THE UNEXPECTED OCCURS

If you and your child are experiencing a difficult family situation, such as a death or divorce, or if you're having to adjust to a new environment as the result of a move, it would be best to delay or ease up on training until the child feels more secure. High levels of stress are not conducive to a successful training experience.

When a child has to deal with an overly-anxious adult, he becomes anxious himself. This type of anxiety produces insecurity with all the trappings. Under such circumstances, there is no need to further burden a child with a consistent training program. Ease up. If training has already begun, sitting your child on the potty when he wakes up in the morning and after naps would be quite acceptable as a temporary arrangement. If this appears to be too much for your child to handle, then stop training for a while.

Keep in mind that it's not uncommon for a child to regress somewhat when living in a highly stressful situation. So don't worry about his losing the control that has already been achieved. It will return. Your child will indicate when he's ready to deal with sitting on a potty again. Be patient. Training is more than achieving control. It's a very personal experience that requires a pleasant atmosphere. If that means waiting for stress to subside, then wait.

STRESS MAY CAUSE A TODDLER TO LOSE ALL CONTROL

Occasionally, highly stressful situations will cause a child who has developed full control to suddenly lose it. This could occur upon the birth of another baby, separation from a parent, major illness or change of houses. This is normal and can even be expected. Some children lose partial control. Others lose all control of their bowels and bladder. Usually, this is only a temporary problem which the child will overcome within a few months. But if your child shows no improvement after several months (especially if a total lack of control has occurred), you should seek help from your pediatrician or a child psychologist.

CYSTITIS

Cystitis is a bladder inflammation that usually causes urinary burning and a frequent and urgent need to pee. Fever is rarely associated with cystitis.

Most physicians assume that the infection is usually the result of improper wiping, from the anal area forward. A urinalysis is necessary in order to determine if your child has this problem. This can be done by collecting urine in a sterile container or by the extraction of urine with the use of a small catheter. This is an easily treatable situation. Infection usually responds to medication (sulfa drugs) within forty-eight hours. Treatment usually takes ten to fourteen days. If your child seems to be experiencing any pain while trying to pee, consult your pediatrician.

BEDWETTERS

Sometimes a parent will become concerned if their potty-trained child occasionally wets the bed. For most, time will usually take care of the problem. There's really no need to be worried, as long as the child seems to be doing fine physically and emotionally.

However, if the child is four years old or older and still wetting the bed, he should be given a thorough physical to rule out any possibility of an organic problem. The majority of children will not have physical problems in this area. But you should check to be sure.

Bedwetting is often the result of a stressful situation within the home. Divorce, separation from a parent, death, a new baby, a move, even beginning pre-school or day-care—all are threatening to a child and create inner conflicts. Threatening or punishing a child *does not* improve the problem. Neither does limiting liquids or forcing the child into the bathroom at all hours. Love and encouragement are usually all that is needed. If you have any doubts about your handling of the problem, don't hesitate to contact a child psychologist for additional input.

FOR THE WORKING PARENT

Potty training is a special concern for parents who take their children to day-care centers. Potty training is really a daytime experience. Children learn more readily when they're awake and alert. You can't expect to train a child only in the evening because he's then tired and becomes easily frustrated. And so are you! Although quality day-care centers can be fine for stimulating a child's educational and social development, few of them contribute to potty training. In fact, you'll be extremely lucky to find any day-care worker who'll care to assist you with your potty training efforts. But do take the time to sit and talk with the people who care for your child during the day. With luck, you'll find an individual who is willing to work with you to personalize the potty training system. But most day-care facilities simply can't take the time for it all.

While it's true that most day-care employees won't even approach potty training, they can be asked to make a special effort to keep your child in dry diapers. The constant feel of a dry diaper encourages your child not to become complacent with the idea of wearing a wet one. This request is not unusual nor inappropriate. You can also ask them to talk to your toddler while changing him, to tell him he has a wet diaper and that they're putting on a dry one. This allows your child to make constant comparisons between being wet and being dry and to learn the distinction between the two words.

If you can't find someone who is willing to help you with the training and feel that now is the time to begin, then you really have only one choice left. You're just going to have to do it all by yourself and work with the time available. The approach will still be the same. In the early weeks, tend to the potty training with every opportunity that comes along. Place your child on his potty as soon as he wakes up and again before you leave for work. At the end of the day, place your tot on his potty again another two or three times.

Take maximum advantage of weekends and days off to continue training. Read this manual again and adapt it as best you can to your own schedule and to your child's. Cooperation from both of you is essential in order for your child to make the step from diapers to underwear. Your attitude is your best asset at this time, so make the most of it.

A FINAL WORD

The key to successful potty training is a stress-free, playful approach. A child learns best when he entertains you as well as himself. He loves games and, most of all, your smiles and enthusiasm. With your help and encouragement, he'll take great pride in sharing this new experience with you. Happy training!

A Private Moment

Index